DISCOVERING JOB JOY

DISCOVERING JOB JOY

YOUR GUIDE TO STRETCHING WITHOUT SNAPPING

#Discover Job Joy

Patti Seda

JONES MEDIA
PUBLISHING

DEDICATION

Everyone needs a tribe. The people in your life that pick you up, dust you off, give you a hug, or a pep talk or just sit and be with you when you need it. The people who also know when you need a kick in the butt to "just do it."

Yes, everyone needs a tribe, and I am beyond blessed to have a few incredible tribes who help make this life possible!

The Greely Girls: five women who have been my best friends, confidants, and therapists for nearly fifty years.

The Women and Wine Group: an eclectic group who have encouraged me to share my passion, expand my business, and write this book.

The One Word Goddesses: we helped each other gain focus, cherish the everyday moments, and open our hearts and souls to what God has in store for each of us.

My Working Mom Mentor (and gut-check editor), Pat: for teaching me you can have a fulfilling career and be a great mom.

My Philanthropic Mentor, Art: for modeling that to whom much is given (and/or is fortunate enough to earn), much is expected.

My Business Mentor, Kim: for providing early guidance that not every hill is worth dying on, what you reinforce is what you get, and has ALWAYS been my trusted advisor!

The Ying to my Yang, Molly: my opposite in almost every way and the ONLY reason all my thoughts landed on paper to help write this book.

And last, but far from least, my husband, Dan: my rock, biggest supporter, and the willing subject of many of the stories in this book. My kids, Nate (and Jenny), Stephanie (and Ben), and Blake (and Peyton), who challenge me in the best ways possible. My sweet granddaughters, Lily, Ellary, and Charlie, who make me giggle and give me perspective on what is really important in life—grandkids do that to you! And my lovable yellow lab, Gus, who is constantly by my side and thinks I'm brilliant and this book is amazing.

Contents

Chapter 1

How I Have to be When I Grow Up

Mrs. Ashline was my third-grade teacher. She was the wife of the banker in our small town and was very prim and very proper. Every day at 8:20, me and my nineteen classmates, thirteen girls and seven boys, were expected to enter the classroom on time and quickly make our way to our desk, one of the twenty that were neatly lined up facing the chalkboard.

I sat at my metal desk, with attached wooden chair, and lifted the top to see everything an eight-year-old would need to be successful: #2 pencils, crayons, lined paper, a few folders, and safety scissors. With my hair neatly tied up in two pig tails that bounced when I skipped, my very best friends around me, and three recesses every day, I loved third grade and all of the time we were allowed to talk, play, and sing songs!

One day, Mrs. Ashline asked us to write a short paper on what we wanted to be when we grew up. Growing up on a farm in our town of 300, my list of possible career choices was pretty short. I could be a farm wife, secretary, receptionist, bank teller, nurse, clerk at the drug store, or a teacher. That day I committed to being a receptionist, where I could meet and greet every human being that entered an office. I don't remember how long I wanted to be a receptionist, but I do remember that question being asked over and over and over again for the next several decades.

We spend most of our lives trying to answer the question, "What do I want to be when I grow up?" This certainly is a great question, and there are plenty of people to give you advice on how to answer it— your parents, school counselors, friends, and siblings. The guidance is usually based on what technical aptitude you exemplify early in life. If you're good at math, you should be an accountant. If you thrive in science, you should be a nurse or a doctor. If you line your dolls up in a row and give them instructions, you should definitely be a teacher.

Throughout this book I'll share some of the different jobs I held— including a receptionist and a bank teller—until I fell into my "calling" of human resources. And it truly is a calling. I cannot stop myself from doing this type of work—on the clock, off the clock, at work, at home, with colleagues, with friends. My mind is all about guiding people, teams, and organizations to be their best.

And yet, even in this role that most days fit me like a custom-made glove, there were times I was so low I thought for sure I had chosen the wrong path. It was so very confusing. Weeks, months, years would go by that I was running on all eight-cylinders, then slowly but surely my energy would be zapped, my performance would be just "acceptable," and I would tell myself, "It's called work for a reason, right?"

With the advantage of hindsight, new insight, and years of experience, I learned that in addition to answering the question about *what I want to be*, we need to be just as vigilant in answering *how* I *have* to be. This second, and equally critical question, relates to how you do the work. The "how" is all about your authentic way of thinking, reacting, working, and communicating. The "how" is not your technical expertise, it's about how you execute your expertise.

The "how" can actually help you refine the position within your career. If you enjoy science and want to get into the medical field, the "how" can you help figure out if you're better suited to be a fast-paced ER doctor, or if your traits are better suited to be an anesthesiologist. If you enjoy computer science, the "how" can provide insight on whether you will have the most joy as a programmer or supervising the team.

Combining the "what" and the "how" is where the magic happens! And that is where you will *Discover Job Joy!*

Life is Like a Rubber Band

If you have a rubber band nearby, pick it up. If there is not one within reach, imagine holding one in your hand. Now, think of managing your career like a rubber band. First, lay that rubber band on the table. What will happen to that rubber band if it just lies there and is not stretched for days? How about if it's not stretched for weeks, months, or even years? At some point it becomes brittle, and even if you try to use it, it will break and no longer be useful.

Next, pull that rubber band as tight as you can; hold it, hold it, hold it! My guess is you're squinting your eyes because you know that if you stretch it for too far for too long, it will eventually snap. And who do you suppose will get hurt when that happens? You! And not only will you get hurt, but anyone in close range will suffer as well.

Now, take that rubber band and pull it tight, then let it spring back. Do that over and over. It feels like a happy rubber band, doesn't it? Just springing back and forth. Getting stretched, then coming back

3

to center to get recharged. In fact, it almost becomes automatic—the more you spring it back and forth, the closer you get to the point where you don't even notice it's happening.

That springing back and forth is where you *Discover Job Joy.*

My career has resembled all stages of that rubber band, and I want to give you the tools, hope, and encouragement to help your career resemble a happy rubber band, where you find joy in what you do. This is the sweet spot where the "what" and the "how" are equally fulfilling. The place where you are equally stretched and allowed to come back to center to recharge. The days where you are challenged but not to the point of snapping, the days where you can rest and recover, and just the right number of days in that sweet spot in between!

I hope you hold onto that rubber band all the while you're reading this book. Be mindful and truthful as to where you are on your journey to Job Joy, and strive every day to be like a happy rubber band.

Chapter 2

STRETCH, DON'T SNAP

Can you think of a time when you were at your best? A time when you felt like you could move mountains and your rubber band was happy?

Some individuals are at their absolute best when they have a long-term project and what they are working on requires very little interaction with their colleagues. For other people, their best is a job portfolio that requires them to engage with multiple groups throughout the day, brainstorming, and developing solutions to complex problems on a very quick timeline.

Both jobs are necessary to the companies these people represent. And if these individuals are in the correct role based on their hardwired personalities, executing these job responsibilities will give them Job Joy.

But how do we know what will give us Job Joy? That's what we will discover in this book!

We spend most of our lives focused on choosing a profession that will make us happy: doctor, teacher, engineer, sales, plumber, etc. Yet, if you're like me, your shelves are filled with self-improvement books. They run the gamut from a book that will make me more efficient to one that will make me more assertive. I even have one that gives a step-by-step process on how to be more likeable by tilting your head to show you trust the person so much you're willing to expose your carotid artery. Yikes!

I have picked up bits and pieces from each of these books, and it has helped to move the needle for me *just a little bit*. But I found I was at my best, had the most energy, was the best leader, wife, mom, grandmother, and community leader when I capitalized on my strengths—the *how*. My strengths are my innate needs—the way I am authentically wired—that drive my behavior. That's when I had the greatest Job Joy.

To help you understand you and understand how we're all different, I will share stories about me, my family, as well as those of clients and colleagues. But here's a primer on me: I am a super creative extrovert with just enough attention to detail to function in my everyday life. When I put all those amazing traits to use every day, I feel like I can change the world. And I have amassed energy reserves to do the things that don't come naturally to me...in small doses. But stick me in front of a computer ALL DAY and there aren't enough Essential Oils in the world to get me off the couch at night.

Discovering Job Joy is at the heart of what my life's work is all about, and I am ecstatic to share it with you.

I'm guessing because you are reading this book you have reached a point where you've started to ask yourself one or more of the following questions:

- How do I get unstuck?
- How can I have a more fulfilling life?
- Why do I have these "huge" feelings about work and my life? Why am I so angry, shameful, or fearful?
- Am I truly passionate about what I do?
- What are my strengths and weaknesses?
- Why do other people I meet seem happier and more fulfilled than me?
- And the mother of all questions: Can I be fixed?

First of all, congratulations! You are asking yourself great questions. These are the same questions I have asked myself and hundreds of clients and colleagues have expressed when they begin their Job Joy journey. Chances are, if you are asking yourself these questions you don't know where to start finding the answers. But your gut is telling you that there are, in fact, answers for the way you are feeling.

OK, I'm listening, so what is Job Joy?

When you are around someone who loves what they do, you can see it, and most likely feel it. This person talks about what they do with passion and purpose. After interviewing and working with thousands of people who have Job Joy and those who are stuck, miserable, and pining for Job Joy, there are a few common themes, regardless of industry or profession:

- Job Joy is NOT about going in late and leaving early. No one ever described being at their best when they weren't stretched. In fact, most people will describe being at their WORST when they weren't stretched, needed, or putting in a meaningful day.
- Job Joy is NOT about a fast pass to retiring early, unless you're literally counting down the days to retirement. In fact, many

people who have great Job Joy are nervous about retiring because they love what they do.

- It's NOT about finding the "perfect" job. With so many options out there and numerous self-help books (and even this book), it's easy to think there's a perfect job. What if, instead, we strive for "imperfectly" perfect? This is where the stretching occurs and where you appreciate the easier days.
- It's NOT about automatically jumping ship just because some parts or all of your current job are in the SNAP moment. It's about recognizing where you are and how to manage your career. Sometimes it means leaving a job and other times it means just making a few adjustments.
- Job Joy IS about looking forward to your next assignment, going to the office, and working with the next client.
- Job Joy IS knowing that what you are doing is meaningful and you were meant to be there!
- Job Joy IS about being in a role you may consider doing even if you didn't get paid. By the way, that's a very small group of people who go that far!
- Job Joy IS about being drawn to doing what you do—this NEED to do what you do. In fact, it probably comes so naturally to you, you assume everyone else can do it and you may not even see it as being that special.

This is your Personal Guide

I've been on the Job Joy journey you are currently on, and I know from first-hand experience it's not easy to admit when something just isn't working in your life. Please know you are not alone. This book is your guide to help begin to understand your authentic self, to accept and *love* your authenticity, maneuver yourself into the right role(s) where you are at your best, and finally, to purposefully manage your Job Joy for the rest of your life!

In the following pages there will be moments when you will be prompted to pause and think about how you are wired. Not how you or someone else in your life thinks you should be, or what you want to be, but who you are authentically. By "authentic" and "wired" I mean the "how" you do your work; your go-to way of thinking, reacting, working, and being. You are encouraged to take notes as you go along, either right in this book, or you can download a PDF of the worksheet from my website: www.PattiSeda.com/DiscoveringJobJoy. Research shows you are five times more likely to retain information if you write it down.

Let's start by reflecting on two extremes in your life. Before you tackle this first assignment, keep these instructions in mind when responding to the questions below:

- Write down the first three things that come to your mind. Don't overthink it.
- Be specific. Reflect on a very specific situation/instance/ example. Generalities are not nearly as effective as specific examples.
- Your example may be an entire job, a project, an assignment, or a task.
- Your example can be a work or volunteer scenario.
- Be completely honest. There is NO judgment! This is for you and only you to reflect upon.

Ok, here we go!

1) When were you at your best? This is a time when you felt unstoppable and meant to do the thing you were doing. Maybe you were drawn to doing it and it may have been harder to NOT do it than it was to dive right in. Or, you were nervous about

doing it, but when it was done you literally (or figuratively) jumped for joy. You were a happy rubber band!

2) Now, when were you at your lowest? A time when you felt stuck, "fine," or even unsuccessful. No matter what you tried (training, hiring a coach, diffusing Essential Oils, enrolled in counseling), you just couldn't get excited about what you were supposed to do. Maybe you reached a level of competence and met the minimum standard but could never break through to excellence or excited about the work. You were either a rubber band that was never stretched or you were stretched to the point of snapping.

Throughout the book we are going to examine various personality traits: how you think, your need to win, what fuels you, how you react to situations, and your relationship with time. At the end of most chapters you will be prompted to complete activities to help clearly identify your unique strengths. It may be helpful to refer back to your "best" and "lowest" list. By the end of this book you will have a better understanding of what makes you authentically you and how to stretch yourself without snapping.

So, grab your rubber band and let's get started on your journey to Job Joy!

Chapter 3

HARDWIRED

Job Joy exists. Hopefully you have experienced at some point, or you have it today. Maybe you are so stuck or stretched right now you couldn't think of an example in the prior chapter. Maybe you never had Job Joy and question whether it exists. Like many of my clients when we first begin working together, you may find yourself saying, "It's called 'work" for a reason, right?"

Job Joy is a term I first heard from Joe, the CEO with whom I worked for many years. As the head of the HR team, I found these two words to be interesting, but I didn't spend a tremendous amount of time pondering Job Joy until I started my consulting business. My re-awakening to Job Joy came after meeting with several clients who struggled with identifying their strengths and that breakthrough moment when they not only understood and accepted their strengths, but came to love what makes them unique. Each of us is hardwired a certain way, yet instead of embracing these unique strengths we may feel shame about what makes us different due to years of people *should-ing* on us.

What do I mean by *should-ing*? I'm sure you've heard it before and would recognize it. The affable boss who says, "You <u>should</u>

be more assertive." The friend who has your best interest in mind when she says, "You <u>should</u> be more sociable." Or the coworker who casually mentions, "You <u>should</u> pick up the pace, we run fast here!" And, of course, the middle school teacher who constantly told you, "You <u>should</u> be quieter!" (Raise your hand if "talks too much" was on EVERY one of your report cards!) There is no shame if you're an avowed extrovert, just as there is no judgment passed if you're a quiet decision maker. It's what makes you authentically amazing. And having this awareness allows you the ability to crank up your traits when it works and temper it just a little when the situation calls for a little less.

This hardwiring includes a variety of factors, notably the level of a person's natural tendency toward creativity, whether you're a take-charge person or one who is focused on doing the work, whether you're geared more toward introversion versus extroversion, whether you're more logical or emotional, and the pace or rate at which you prefer to work.

The hardwiring of who you are and how you work—your personality, strengths, and weaknesses—are baked in from the time you are born, through your formative teenage years, until you're pretty much "fully baked" by the time you're a young adult.

My personal *aha!* moment came when I was in a role where I just couldn't succeed. My natural way of working, communicating, and thinking that had helped me succeed in the past were now working against me. It took a long time for me to understand and accept my authentic self in a way I had never understood. And it formed the basis of the actions I took to begin to feel fulfilled and happy. This was a journey of self-discovery for me, and although it's an audacious goal, I'm writing to make this world a better place…one joyful employee at a time. My goal is to create more joyful employees who have had such great days their energy spills over into their personal life. They operate from a place of abundance and want to lift others up to their fullest potential.

Conversely, I have yet to meet someone who had a terrible day at the office and greets their family with, "Oh, I'm so glad to be home! I love my family and want to know everything about your day." Nope. A terrible day at the office spills right into your personal life. If the dog runs the other way when you walk in the door, it's time to get serious about discovering your Job Joy!

What I have learned is simple: To have a balanced, fulfilled, and happy professional and personal life, you must know your authentic self and operate within these inherent strengths.

Once you operate with an understanding of your authentic strengths, it makes it possible for you to occasionally operate within your weaknesses. But, don't spend too much time there or you'll snap. You need to be cognizant of what your strengths are so you recognize when you're not in that role or "sweet spot." You must manage and be aware of your strengths.

A Slow Road to Misery

Let me explain to you what was happening in my life that started me on the path to Job Joy.

I was 48 years old and had been with my company for nearly 25 years. My career had been an upward trajectory since my early twenties. I was blessed to be in the right place at the right time, doing mostly the right things and working with really good people. Then I decided to take a leap and see if I could do it again. I wanted to help grow another company by leading the people strategy. I was confident this role aligned with my strengths and would allow me to stretch myself for the final hurrah of my working career!

The job started out great. Like most new employees, there was a "honeymoon" period in which everything was rosy. It wasn't until about two months into the new position that a tiny voice in the back of my head whispered, "Something isn't quite right." Having just changed jobs and needing to be gainfully employed, I did what most hardworking, company-focused employees are trained to do. I ignored that voice and soldiered on.

By the fourth month in my new job, I was seeing a chiropractor a few times a week. The knots in my shoulders and cricks in my back would not go away. Those few seconds in my chiropractor's office were pure heaven. I would feel relief, only to have that feeling dashed away in the span of less than an hour. Normally a very healthy person, I started getting repeated colds. On the advice of several girlfriends, I invested in a variety of Essential Oils. I had diffusers in every room of my house and my office at work. My kids joked that I had started an apothecary! And yes, I certainly had more than a few glasses of Chardonnay.

But I could not get over the feeling I had hit a wall. Physically, I could barely get through the day at work. Meetings—especially in-person meetings in which I was typically at my best—were torture. Once the workday was mercifully finished, I would drive the twenty minutes to my home, always my haven and safe place in the past. With our youngest just about to graduate from high school, I was on autopilot for the nightly routine. I'd make dinner, ask about homework, ask my son and husband about their days, feed the dog, plop onto the couch to stare at my computer, and just generally try to make it to ten o'clock, which I deemed an acceptable hour to go to bed. I would collapse into bed. But I would wake numerous times during the night, fretting about what was to come at work the next day.

I kept thinking, *This is crazy, I am doing the same type of work and have been successful, what is wrong with me?* When you're "in it" it's hard to think logically and realize not all jobs are created equal when you factor in a different industry, different colleagues, and a very different supervisor.

My family interactions were suffering. Add to that the fact I had previously benefited from a network of trusted colleagues at my former place of employment, and I was reeling. My workplace safety net had been replaced by a feeling of not belonging to the pack at my new employer. I remember that feeling as a young child of walking into the school cafeteria and worrying that no one would invite me to have lunch with them at their table. That was my new reality at work. Every. Single. Day.

Something had to change. What I didn't fully grasp at the time is the science behind personality, including inherent strengths and weaknesses. People situated in the wrong role—a role that doesn't allow them to use their strengths—suffer physically, mentally, and emotionally. Understanding and accepting the science behind this ultimately led me on my journey of finding my true self and becoming a fulfilled, happy person.

On the Shoulders of Giants

Let's geek out for a moment to understand the science behind the hardwiring. Along with personal and professional observations, it's important to note there is a wealth of research about the psychology of personality.

The interest in discovering what makes people behave a certain way was first documented in the time of Ancient Greece. Hippocrates, Plato, and Aristotle all delved into the science behind personality psychology. Much credit is given to Fourth Century BCE philosopher Hippocrates as the first to suggest a "four factors" theory of temperament, theorizing individuals have either a hot or cold and moist or dry make-up of their personality. Plato and Aristotle would eventually adapt this early "four factors" personality theory to traits such as artistic, sensible, intuitive, and reasoning. These observations laid the groundwork for discussions about temperament and the connections between the physical aspects of the body and behavior, which would then advance rapidly with research in the pre-World War II era.

In the 1960s, the Big Five personality traits concept was advanced by Ernest Tupes and Raymond Christal, but it failed to reach a wider audience until the 1980s. The Big Five factors consist of:

- *Openness to experience (inventive/curious vs. consistent/ cautious)*
- *Conscientiousness (efficient/organized vs. easy-going/careless)*
- *Extraversion (outgoing/energetic vs. solitary/reserved)*
- *Agreeableness (friendly/compassionate vs. challenging/detached)*
- *Neuroticism (sensitive/nervous vs. secure/confident)*

Most current personality assessment tools and research is based on the Big Five factors. If you're a science enthusiast, it's easy to get lost in the studies and the latest research. If you're wired more like me, you appreciate the *Reader's Digest* version of the science behind personality!

Focusing on and understanding the fact that there is science behind what makes a person who he or she is was the catalyst for me changing my life, ultimately discovering Job Joy, and becoming a happier person. It provided the scientific bedrock for me to begin to understand and celebrate my inherent strengths.

Snapping Back

As we continue through this book, I will reference our happy rubber band and the place where we are all at our best—when we are bouncing back and forth between being stretched and in recovery mode.

Most chapters of this book include personal stories of clients, colleagues, friends, and some family members. At the end of each story, you'll start to notice I occasionally include SNAP or STRETCH at the end of the vignette. I hope you'll pay attention to this clue, and even incorporate it into your daily lexicon. When you're at work and the role you are doing isn't bringing you Job Joy, you may start to recognize a SNAP moment. Conversely, when you're in your sweet spot, I hope you start to think STRETCH.

We will spend the next few chapters discussing why Job Joy is important, beyond the obvious factors, and how we can all get closer to being happy little rubber bands.

Chapter 4

More than Joy

Job Joy is about more than just bouncing around like a happy rubber band.

Stress eventually affects us mentally, physically, and/or emotionally. For me, it showed up as a pain in my back. But let's start at the beginning.

As a fairly goal-oriented person, I had set my sights on achieving a certification in my field. I became obsessed with this goal. I poured a lot of time, energy, and mental capacity into studying for this exam. I had convinced myself that passing this certification was the end-all be-all to my career. In looking back, it was more about my ego and proving to myself, and others, I could pass this test. I studied the better part of a family vacation, and about halfway through started getting a pain in my back that wouldn't go away. I cried for the better part of the six-hour drive home trying to get comfortable. Once again, I got out the Essential Oils, had a two-hour massage, and drank a glass (or three) of wine. SNAP.

The next day the pain disappeared with a simple click of a button.

The button was actually the "submit" key on the test. And the pain disappeared when I saw that I passed. It was that fast—and I literally skipped out of the test center.

During a workshop on this topic of how stress can lead to pain, a young lady in her thirties approached me in tears. She shared she had terrible stomach issues and doctors struggled to diagnose it and finally labeled it IBS: Irritable Bowel Syndrome. She told me the pain started a few months before she got married, disappeared a month after her divorce was finalized. Once she felt better she looked back during the time she was married and realized it was always worse as she got closer to the weekend, and got a little better on Monday. Of course, the advantage of hindsight made this incredibly clear, but was not obvious when she was in the middle of it.

I'm not saying that Job Joy is the answer to cancer, or that everyone who has IBS has a deep-rooted issue to resolve. What I am saying is unresolved stress can manifest itself in our body, usually the head, neck, or torso (rarely do we get a pain in our pinky finger when we're stressed). And physical ailments are often traced back to a stress we are experiencing in our lives.

The bottom line is simple: If you lack joy, you don't have to live this way!

Let's repeat that again: If you lack joy, you don't have to live this way!

And, once more, for those of us who are hardheaded: If you lack joy, you don't have to live this way!

In fact, you should NOT live this way!

Let me tell you a little bit about a former client named Mary and the transformation that occurred in her life with first some understanding of her inherent strengths and some relatively small adjustments in her work.

I first met Mary when I was invited by her company's CEO to address the productivity gaps she felt existed in their business. I completed assessments with the top-level management at the organization and compared their profiles with that of their job descriptions. I was stunned that Mary, an unabashed perfectionist, was in the role of supervising a large number of people. I had not previously met Mary, so following our profile assessment and conversation, I asked her to show me around her office.

Mary is a very quiet person and an introvert. The office she brought me to looked much like a therapist's office or spa waiting room. The lights were low, there was calming music playing, and the shades were drawn. If it hadn't been against fire code, Mary probably would've been burning incense and candles! She had manufactured the entire setting in order to provide a calm, peaceful setting for her work. I loved this!

But there was one flaw: it wasn't working. Mary put on a brave face and said all the right things about managing people. She sought to provide high-level guidance, give them the autonomy to do their work, celebrate their successes, and offer them great feedback when they needed it.

But our conversation seemed very scripted...because it was. Mary knew exactly what she *should* be doing, and she tried so very hard to do it. Yet, when I posed the first question I ask every client, "Describe a time when you were at your best," she said nothing about leading, managing, or even being around people. Her eyes lit up when she talked about audits and analyzing and immersing herself in computer work. After a few minutes, Mary confided, "I'm not sure how much more I can take." This revelation was the first foray into a deep dive about Mary's profile and the position she was in at a company she adored. She disclosed that for nearly a year, ever since being thrust into this role at her firm, she was suffering intense migraines. These migraines were so terrible they would knock her out of work for multiple days. She needed to have complete silence and darkness in order to recover. This was why she had created her calming office environment! SNAP!

Mary's direct reports liked her, and most respected her, but they were also afraid to bring issues to her, knowing her history with migraines and being fearful any sort of stress would trigger them. They were being great teammates and looking out for her—without fully understanding the fact that having direct reports was part of her issue!

My conversation with Mary's supervisor uncovered there was a need for someone to do all the audit, analyzing, and computer work. Through this simple "let's get real" conversation with employee and employer, Mary, a perfectionist, was moved into a role that required her to be a perfectionist, but without direct reports. Instead, she would be a "deep specialist." Mary excelled at the details of a project and relished being the person to whom people came for advice and direction. She just didn't want them to report to her!

Within a week of Mary's shift in responsibilities, she had far fewer migraines. And additionally, she didn't feel the need to keep her office lights dimmed and shades drawn! In this new capacity, she was eager to interact with her co-workers, on a limited basis, and offer her expertise in a well-lit environment! STRETCH!

Correlation between Misery and Pain on a Larger Scale

I've also witnessed this premonition in large groups. When working for a company that was experiencing tremendous growth, high retention of clients and employees, and low absenteeism; we were winning in every measurable business category. People loved coming to work.

Then came the economic crash in 2008 and the start of the decline in revenue and eventual cutbacks. Work got harder. People began to experience pressure they never had before. And in the middle of this, I received a call from the COO. He asked why everyone in a certain department in a certain location had migraines, insinuating we were purposefully finding the sickest people in the community and plopping them smack dab in his department. From the outside, I could see why it appeared that way.

We began to look at the absenteeism and found many of the days off were on Monday, which of course prompted the questions:

- Was it a weekend hangover when they missed work on Monday?
- Were our employees dreading work so much on Sunday night that they were legitimately sick on Monday?
- Was it likely that some people were faking it or gaming the system?

In our analysis and interviews with employees, we discovered employees in certain departments expressed higher levels of stress based on a variety of reasons: long hours, more pressure to perform more work with less people, an uncaring/unsupportive supervisor. There was direct correlation between high stress and high absenteeism/turnover. And, while the supervisor wanted to blame the employees for being lazy or unreliable, there was a stronger argument that people were physically ill on Sunday/Monday with the increase stress they felt preparing to go to work.

The next time you feel stressed, take your temperature—literally and figuratively. High stress causes a drop in our immune system, and all those germs can jump in and take over!

Now, let's review what happens in most workplace environments. Back to our first example, Mary would have likely continued in her current supervisory role with the company until she decided she couldn't handle it anymore and quit. Or, worse yet, she would have mentally quit but continued to show up for work and would potentially have been fired.

Under either scenario, her company would have lost a very valuable, committed employee without fully understanding that she was a *great employee in the wrong role.*

For every "Mary" there may be thousands more who are plugging away in a role for which they are ill suited, but either don't know why or how to disentangle themselves from it. The key is to remember there are always choices! If you lack joy and are unfulfilled, you don't have to live this way!

Think of operating within your authentic strengths like using an escalator. When you run down a "down" escalator you can reach your destination much more quickly; you're running with the intended strengths of the escalator. Conversely, when you're running against the escalator, you're working against the mechanics. It's hard. It takes so much longer. And if you're on the outside looking in, it looks ridiculous.

Similarly, your job should not be like running against the escalator. And, I'm assuming since you picked up this book, you're feeling a little like that right now. Kudos to you for taking the first step to stop the madness and getting on the escalator moving in the right direction to Job Joy!

Chapter 5

How You Think

It's time to dig into understanding these unique strengths that will bring Job Joy and are the key to overall happiness and well being!

Let's start with creativity, something many don't think about when it comes to personality traits. We all talk about the need to be creative and innovative, but many don't realize that at the core, some people are "inside the box" thinkers, and others, well, they have thrown the box away. That's how far "outside the box" they are!

When I think of creativity, I recall my work in helping a tax team prepare to navigate the hectic tax season.

Sounds odd, right? Taxes and creativity aren't typically uttered in the same sentence, unless we're talking about Enron. When I ask my accountant to complete my family's taxes in April (yes, I tend to "thrive in the deadline" with everything, even my taxes!), I do not want them to be *overly creative*. When I envision an *overly creative* tax person, I see them marching in an orange prison jumpsuit with me marching closely behind them!

However, my opportunity to lead a workshop on team building and communication for a tax team reminded me that, as with every trait, we need a balance of think-outside-the box thinkers and those who are more pragmatic. Having this balance ensures we're not reinventing the wheel. Every. Single. Time.

The tax firm's senior leadership team asked me to lead a workshop that would help identify and maximize the strengths of each team member in order to build stronger communications, and identify how to "raise a red flag" in an appropriate, meaningful manner when stressed. Basically, we would devise strategies to work together to ensure they did not hate each other at the end of the incredibly stressful, intensive tax season. Stress sometimes brings out the best, but often accentuates the worst in all of us.

During the teambuilding session, it became apparent there was awkwardness between a supervisor and her direct report. The tension was all about creativity and where each employee fell within this broad range.

Through the teambuilding session, I was introduced to Barbara, a partner whose creativity is off-the-charts. She loves working one-on-one with clients to solve complex issues. Her mind is constantly churning out new ideas like it's a Cuisinart blender. I loved working with her because we are closely aligned on the spectrum of creativity and we believe that the more ideas, the better.

As with many managers or partners who have been with a firm for a long time, Barbara had acquired several direct reports. They all agreed she was a good boss: open, consistent, helpful, and always had their backs.

However, there was one of Barbara's direct reports, Sally, who just wasn't feeling the love. She felt increasingly anxious by Barbara's creativity, ideation sessions, and never-ending ideas. But Sally was new to the firm and was keen to please both her boss and her clients—as we all know that is the way to get that next big promotion. So, she, like many others, suffered in silence.

Until our workshop.

With every coaching session or workshop, I always start with the first step of identifying the personality traits (aka: strengths) of each team member. And the chart at the front of the room called out in neon lights that Barbara was an off-the-charts creative thinker. And it also showed clearly that Sally was a very pragmatic, do-it-by-the-book accountant. I told stories of the opposite ends of the spectrum in that pragmatic thinkers are more "by the proven methods" folks and creative thinkers live, work, and play "outside the box." While there was quiet chatter in the room (this was a room filled with mostly introverts, so it never got too loud or out of control), Barbara's and Sally's eyes got wider and wider.

Barbara turned to Sally and said, "Those client meetings where we need to find new and different ways of tackling a problem must drive you crazy!" Sally, with tears welling up in her eyes, slowly nodded. "I really just want to sit in my office and apply all that I learned in college to crank out tax returns." This thought never occurred to Barbara. Because she hated following the pragmatic, tried-and-true ways of doing things, she assumed everyone else would hate that, too.

But, not Sally. As a young new graduate, Sally thrived in a role in which she could apply the proven, successful way of doing things. It was not her personality to identify seven different solutions to a

29

complex problem. Rather, she wanted to know the proven method and then execute that plan—which she always did flawlessly.

When she and Barbara would meet with clients, Sally couldn't understand why Barbara would present multiple options on a project. It was driving her crazy that the proven, reliable method that had worked very well for other clients was not immediately identified as "the solution." Sally would get pains in her stomach and would have to brace herself to attend meetings with Barbara because she knew the ideation sessions would be endless. She began to wonder if she wasn't smart enough for her job. Sally was constantly asking herself, "What is wrong with me?" SNAP!

Did Barbara and Sally have a terrible partner-direct report relationship? No! They just reside on opposite sides of the creativity chart. Once we were able to identify this vast difference in their makeup, they each began to understand where the other was coming from. For Barbara, it was the realization the back-and-forth slinging of ideas in meetings was often overwhelming for Sally to process, both because of her bend on creativity and because she was a relatively new employee. Sally's sweet spot is going with the tried and true method, and if she gets a big healthy dose of that kind of work on a regular basis, she can occasionally get comfortable with new ideas. But flip the ratio, and her palms start to sweat. The greatest "aha moment" was when they both came to understand the other was not trying to be difficult or intentionally trying to make the other crazy. Barbara and Sally just had a completely different starting point.

The ability to have open, honest discussions about where each of them falls on the scale of creativity was eye opening for both. As they both became more sensitive to one another's natural, authentic strengths, they could also appreciate the different styles of creativity they bring to their team.

As this all unfolded the rest of the team started to listen in. As they learned more about one another and we took this breakthrough back to the stressed-out tax team, it opened the door for another employee, Brad, to raise his hand and say, "Take me"! Like Sally, Brad had been in his office banging out tax return after tax return. But, unlike Sally, this repetitive processing was killing him and his creativity! He longed to go with Barbara to the client meetings to discuss creative ideas to complex tax solutions! The open communication about how to work best as a team revealed other team members' strengths and career desires. STRETCH!

Myth Buster

An interesting facet of the real-life example with Barbara and Sally is that it refutes the idea that creativity is a factor of age. Barbara is in the twilight of her career and ranks high on the chart of creativity. She needs it to thrive! Conversely, Sally is in her mid-twenties but longs for the tried-and-true pragmatic approach to work. A lot of people assume if you're older than fifty you're not creative. Similarly, they assume the young, energetic, recent college graduate *must* be creative. Both are false! Creativity has nothing to do with age!

Let's also refute another assumption. Many people believe incorrectly that creativity is tied to certain industries or professions. It's easy to assume all marketing people are creative types and all accountants are not. The reality is, I've met creative accountants, sales reps, human resource professionals, secretaries, project managers, CEOs, and real estate agents. And I have met just as many people in each of these professions who lean more pragmatic. The primary key to success is to know which one you are so you can seek out someone with the opposite strength when you need a different viewpoint.

When I think of creativity, I immediately think of the significant push in today's world to "think outside the box" and be innovative thinkers. For some individuals, "outside the box" is their playground; a place to explore all the possibilities, the new ideas, the ways to improve whatever is broken or not broken. In some cases, it can be a challenge and a bit frustrating to land on one idea, because the brain keeps "one-upping" that idea.

For others, there's a reason why there is a box. The box contains all the proven ways that work. Best practices are kept in the box, and all you have to do is look in the box to figure out the best way to move forward. These individuals are prone to ask, "Why in the world should we reinvent the wheel/process/recipe/house design/decorating idea... Every. Single. Day?"

Like with every trait, we need people who are pragmatic and those who are creative. Each brings tremendous value to the world. And the more they can play in or out of the "box," the better they can appreciate, understand, and dip their toe in the other side.

Take a few moments to review the Job Joy chart and evaluate where you fall in the broad range of creativity. As with every trait, be honest! Think of others around you and how your creativity compares to theirs, not in a competitive way, but realistically. Is it where you thought you would fall on the creativity chart? Why or why not? In my experience, more issues arise in the workplace with a poor fit on creativity or a misunderstanding of a colleague's creative nature, so I urge you to understand where you are on the spectrum and how it relates to your current role.

What would make you snap? (Circle all that apply to you)	
• Trying something new that hasn't been proven. • Brainstorming when there's a pragmatic/tried-and-true way of doing something.	• Having to abide by "if it's not broke, don't fix it". • When you suggest a new idea, you are told to go back and review the manual/process.
What is your preference? (Circle all that apply to you)	
• Referring to what has worked in the past. • You're known as the "go-to" person for the precedent that was set. • You find yourself struggling to come up with a new idea when the tried-and-true won't work.	• Trying a new idea. • You're the go-to person if everyone is out of ideas. • You find yourself saying, "There is a way to solve this problem, let's keep throwing ideas against the wall".
If you circled more on this side, you're likely more Pragmatic	**If you circled more on this side, you're likely more Creative**
Consider Roles	
• That allow you to spend time applying the proven ways of doing things. • In which new ways of doing things would actually make the outcome worse. • That have strict protocols (such as medical or accounting).	• Where innovation is truly required. • That value process improvement. • In a start-up company where there's no playbook and everything's new.
Ways to stretch yourself	

• Occasionally try a new way of doing things. If this makes you nervous, try something that has low risk or is low profile.
• Phone-a-creative-friend when the established approach isn't working, and you need a new idea.
	• When your mind is racing with a number of ideas, either:
	  – Pick the top three and make a pros/cons list for each, then decide. When things start to go awry, look at your list and see if you identified that as a potential "con." If you did, give yourself a pat on the back for thinking it through and staying on course.
	  – Phone-a-pragmatic-friend to find a balanced approach.
	• Every morning list two things for which you are grateful. At the end of the day, gratitude often brings acceptance that what you have is often enough.

Chapter 6

THE NEED TO WIN

How badly do you need to win?

This is the personality component that often makes me giggle. People's "need to win" characteristics are so abundantly clear—subconsciously—that they can't hide their true colors even if they try! However, not everyone can admit where they fall on the "need to win" scale, even if it is clear to their family or colleagues.

There are two extremes on this "need to win" scale:

- Win at all costs. This person must win at all costs, no matter if their personal or professional relationships are jeopardized in "the victory." This may be a conscious or unconscious decision, by the way.
- Win, lose, or draw. This person is more agreeable and their need to win is far less important than the need and desire for everyone to get along.

Let's delve a bit more deeply into these two extremes.

For those who must win at all costs, the desire to win is always their primary goal. In business and life, it is imperative to these folks their idea is the one that is selected to present to management, their version of the draft is chosen, and they are recognized by the C-Suite as having orchestrated the best idea, or the highest sales. The need to win is their driving force.

You can tell someone has a high need to win by the way they speak. If you have a friend, colleague, or family member who you think has a "win at all costs" personality, pay close attention to the way he or she speaks. Does the person use "I" a lot? If so, it's likely he or she has a high need to win personality. These folks have an innate need to take control. If they are not in charge, they are likely uncomfortable. (And they are probably brainstorming ways in which they can gain control!)

High need to win personalities are also risk takers. They don't take no as the final answer. They tend to be strong in sales because they believe they have the best product or service, and the person who said no to their proposal simply doesn't understand this is exactly what they need. Rejection and confrontation are simply seen as challenges and a welcome and expected part of life.

Conversely, there are those who just want everyone to get along. These people may be introverts or extroverts, but their primary goal is to avoid conflict. When they speak, note that much of their conversational style is peppered with "we" statements. These people are agreeable individuals who tend to go with the flow. And they are very uncomfortable with confrontation or a stressful environment.

Throughout my career I've conducted countless team building sessions where it's clear two colleagues are at opposite ends of the "need to win" spectrum. Here are some strategies for dealing with people who may be at the other end of the scale than you.

My advice to the more agreeable people is to figure out your line in the sand. If you're not clear on your expectations or goals, the super assertive people will believe that you can't or won't make a decision, and they are happy to step in to make it for you. If you're an agreeable person and don't push back, the need to win people assume you're okay with them taking control. It's easy for more agreeable people to feel taken for granted or railroaded. They are more likely to grin and bear it than confront a colleague or friend about an idea with which they disagree.

It is also important to note that agreeableness, over time, can have severe negative impacts mentally, physically, and emotionally. Self-sacrifice—the interest in putting others' wishes before your own wellbeing—can lead to burnout and declining productivity. In a study of 194 nurses (48.5 males and 51.5% females), it was found that "burnout symptoms (emotional exhaustion, depersonalization, and reduced personal accomplishment) were hypothesized to occur among male and female nurses who…feel they invest more in their relationships with patients than they receive in return." [Published in the *Journal of Applied Social Psychology* in 1992]. The net is this: if you only fill someone else's bucket, yours will soon be empty and you'll be resentful!

Regardless of the profession, or if this is a personal or professional relationship, you need to set boundaries and monitor it closely. The only thing worse than allowing someone to take advantage of you, is stuffing those negative feelings over a long period of time then unleashing years of hurt on that person when they hit your last nerve. Your silence is often perceived as your acceptance of their behavior. Pouting or passive aggressive behavior is seen as a reflection on you, and most people will not translate that back to what they could've done to cause you to act that way.

As with all variations on the personality characteristics discussed in this book, there is value in having both need to win and agreeable people on your team. The key is ensuring that each person maintains a healthy respect for the other.

I recently worked with a team of 25 employees who wanted to find ways to improve their working and communication strategies. After completing an assessment of each employee, it was discovered 75% were highly assertive—this was their strongest personality trait. Of the 25 people, 18 needed to be right and needed to win. It was not surprising there was so much contention within this team. With this new awareness, they agreed to do a better job of staying in their own lane and refrain, or at least dial back, from telling others what to do and how to do it.

Let's reflect on a history lesson on a high-risk adventure. My guess is that in 1961 many people thought President John F. Kennedy was in outer space himself when he declared before a special joint session of Congress the dramatic and ambitious goal of sending an American safely to the moon before the end of the decade. President Kennedy had his reasons for wanting to land someone on the moon, which sounded a lot like a "need to win" over the Soviet Union in the Space Race, but he wasn't careless in this bold statement. According to the National Aeronautics and Space Administration (NASA) History Office, he had consulted with Vice President Johnson, NASA Administrator James Webb, and other officials before declaring this goal. Once this idea was made public, there was an enormous human effort and expenditures to make what became Project Apollo a reality by 1969. Make no mistake, President Kennedy and other "need to win" people didn't make this mission happen alone. It took hundreds, possibly thousands, of people who were committed to the detail, who were risk-averse, to ensure not only did someone land on the moon, but also returned safely to Earth…specifically the United States.

At Work and At Home

The need to win personality type looms large in my family and is never more evident than on family game nights. Family game nights are a treasured activity in many families. As they say, families that play together, stay together. Maybe. My professional advice is this adage may not be true for every family. Indeed, you should analyze whether family game night is the right thing for your family. I hope my family game night stories can be instructive for you and your family! Proceed with caution!

From the time my kids were able to understand and independently play board games, around the time when they were all over seven years old, family game nights have been a tradition. The game Trouble was the first to enter the scene. This was obviously a sign of what lay ahead.

If we review our need to win spectrum, I am a high center. I don't enjoy losing, but I don't have to win. My goal with family game night is to have a nice evening where we can all catch up on life while engaging in a pleasant activity. Every other person in my family, which includes a spouse and three children, must win. At. All. Costs. They truly believe the credo, "second place is the first loser."

Throughout the years, I've tried to moderate which games we play in an effort to scale back the need to win that permeates the event. For me, the ultimate worst games to play with my family are those in which a player can sabotage their opponent. They thrive on it. It stresses me out. This is the reason why I have thrown away the game Catan!

It has been interesting to observe the dynamic now that three of my children have brought their spouses/girlfriend into our nearly defunct family game night. For the most part, they are not in the super assertive, must win category. You can see the spouses physically move back from the table when it gets crazy. Family members leaning in, yelling at each other to trade wood for sheep in a fictional society (Catan) is where I draw the line. There's a point at which the need to win can deteriorate relationships. SNAP! However, my husband and children vehemently disagree. Anyone see the irony in those last two statements as it relates to the "need to win," aka the "need to be right?"

Let's Go West! (Did someone pack the food?)

When thinking about the need to win characteristic, I like to recall the Pioneers who explored the West. Until the early 1800s, white settlers had not explored the western portion of the United States. There were no roads and no provisions along the way. It was a completely unknown territory!

Imagine what it took for someone to say, in spite of all of this, "Let's go West!" The Pioneers did not know what lay west of the Mississippi River, but an assertive, high risk person thought, *Let's find out!* Meriwether Lewis and William Clark were tasked by President Thomas Jefferson to explore the lands that comprised the Louisiana Purchase. You can bet Lewis and Clark's need to win personality characteristic was very high! They had considerable assistance from Native Peoples along their journey, but that does not discount the fact there were still countless unknowns and high risk.

But as I cautioned before, need to win people are smart to surround themselves with agreeable people who are more risk averse. In keeping with our metaphor, the agreeable "I Don't Have to Win" folks are going to take care of everything else on the exploration journey. They are the people on the team who will declare, "I have the map!" "I packed the food!" "I have researched the best time to leave and when we should start to hunker down for the night." Thank heavens for these people, without whom the explorers could have been lost, starving, or worse!

From a career perspective, those with a high need to win personality trait typically struggle more than others when they first enter the workforce. Their need to be in control, take the lead, and take risks makes for a challenging employee to manage. It takes a strong manager/leader who also enjoys risk to know how to channel this energy and how to get the newbie to slow down, listen, and understand there are probably others who can add tremendous value and insight that need to be considered, all without squelching their passion and enthusiasm. But, once these people find their sweet spot, they will charge forward and move mountains. Assuming someone packed them a lunch...

The need to win is innate—like all of the other personality characteristics discussed in this book—and the ability to recognize where you fall on this need to win scale will benefit you in the business environment and in life, including the dynamics of family game night!

What would make you snap? (Circle all that apply to you)	
• Sales calls where statistically you are likely to be rejected at least 50% of the time. • Delegating work and allowing the person to do it however they want.	• Being told what to do and exactly how to do it. • Always taking the safe route. • Completing the details for the person who is in charge.
What is your preference? (Circle all that apply to you)	
• Knowing what to expect. • Knowing all the details/the plan before starting a project. • Supporting the team to achieve the score/outcome.	• Charging forward with a new opportunity where the details are figured out as you go, or by someone else. • Primarily responsible for the score/outcome. • Difficulty settling on one idea because there are so many ideas out there.
If you circled more on this side, you're likely more Agreeable	**If you circled more on this side, you're likely more Assertive**
Consider Roles	
• That support the team goal. • Allow you to execute on the details.	• Where you are responsible for your own goals. • Offer you the opportunity to take a chance/take a risk. • Work with people who can support you in the details.
Ways to stretch yourself	
• Occasionally take on a project where all the details aren't planned. If this makes you nervous, start with something that is low-risk and build from there. • When you find yourself nervous when something isn't well planned out, make a list of the worst thing that could happen—make sure it's realistic—and how you would do it! Often, our fear of the unknown can be eased by looking at the worst-case scenario and realizing it isn't that bad.	• Take time to understand the details of a project so you understand what it takes to execute on a big idea. • Ask, and really listen, to those who are taking care of the details if they have all the information they need to move forward. Don't gloss it over or call them a Debbie Downer. If you mentally can't get to that level of detail, find someone who can help bridge the gap. • Express your appreciation to those who take care of the details. They are often behind the scenes and the unsung heroes that bring the big ideas to fruition.

Chapter 7

WHAT FUELS YOU?

The year was 1985. I had worked for about a year as a bank teller. I loved the customers and was good at math, so I was soon recognized as a "good" employee. My reward was a promotion to the accounting department, where I rotated through various duties until one day when I landed in the CD Rate Accrual Department. In the basement. In the corner. All by myself.

Now, let me remind you this was 1985, long before smart phones, flip phones, or desktop computers. To accurately accrue the interest on CDs, my job was to stand up, walk to the row of filing cabinets, take out ten CDs at a time, return to my desk, calculate the interest that was earned since last month, pull out the CDs that would expire the next month, mark the accrual on the general ledger, walk back to the filing cabinet, refile the CDs that would not be expiring (unlike my brain, which expired by 9:00 a.m.), take out the next ten CDs, and start the process all over again.

I can't remember if that job lasted one week, one month or a decade—it's all a blur. I do remember trying to tell my supervisor, Kay, about all the new and different ways we should perform these mind-numbing tasks. At this point her eyes quickly darted my way and she said, while holding up one finger, "Once you master the task and (now holding up the next – middle finger, which I think she secretly wanted to hold up that finger first) perform it accurately, we can then talk about different ways to complete this very important work."

What fuels me is being around people, talking with people, and helping people. What fuels Kay—who I plan to find and apologize for the weeks, months, or years that I must have made her life miserable—is working alone.

Asking "What fuels you?" is akin to asking, "Where do you draw your energy?" This falls into one of two camps: working with and being around people with a lot of external stimuli or working alone with internal/brain stimuli. This is also known as extroversion versus introversion. Extroverts are "talk to thinkers"; they have to say their thoughts out loud to arrive to their final answer. Introverts "think to talk"; they quietly think through the answer and only say their final answer, leaving extroverts to wonder what steps they took to get there!

As we examine these extremes, remember it is imperative for business leaders from the front desk to the corner office to understand where and how they recharge. Each employee's happiness and productivity in business—and in life—often rests on whether they are feeling properly fueled.

Think of "fuel" as the "where and with who/what" you draw your energy. If you are in the right "where" and "who/what," you'll feel like you can move mountains. If you're not, then you won't. You'll be exhausted or depressed. And no one is at their best when they are exhausted or depressed.

A few personal and professional stories have reminded me how crucial understanding what fuels you is to find your Job Joy.

Understanding What Fuels You

I first met Janet through a mutual friend. We clicked immediately, as we are very much alike in terms of values, community-mindedness, and our need to help people be successful. Janet had recently left a job due to a "misalignment of values" with her supervisor. She went from loving what she was doing to dreading her job every single day. Her family was financially sound, so with the encouragement of family and friends, she decided to resign and spend more time with her kids while they were still young.

From the outside looking in, Janet's life looked amazing. She didn't have the stress of a high-pressure job, she could volunteer, spend time with her kids, her parents, and her friends. She could do what she wanted to when she wanted to do it. But the more time I spent with Janet, the more I could see past the façade.

In the grand scheme of things in terms of poverty, war, food scarcity, and homelessness, Janet's life was amazing. She and her family were not facing any of these issues. She fully owned this and felt guilty implying otherwise. But something was terribly off, and she just couldn't figure it out. She was silently depressed, which made her feel even guiltier, given others' view of her life.

Janet is a complete extrovert. On a scale of one to ten, she's an eleven. She gets all her energy from being around people and helping to solve their problems. This isn't just a "let's meet to have coffee and talk about problems at the school" need. Janet has an innate need to help people with complex business issues. When that need is not met, she loses energy. She literally can't get off the couch.

Janet plowed through the summer, doing small project work and spending time with her family. She cherished all these opportunities.

But, it hit her like a brick when she turned the calendar and saw the "First Day of School." She felt punched in the gut.

Her inner monologue said, "That's the first day of being alone. Again."

Janet knew she had to make a change. She needed to draw every ounce of energy she could muster, get off the couch, walk confidently into an interview, and show the new potential employer what she could bring to their firm. All of this took tremendous effort, given her confidence was severely rocked and her fuel tank was close to empty.

Once she got into the interview and started sharing her knowledge, her fuel tank meter started to go up. First slowly, then very quickly. Through her relentless perseverance, Janet landed a great job and started it shortly after the kids started school.

I saw Janet the week before she started, and there was literally a spring in her step. She sat up a little taller when she talked about this new role. She knows there will be really hard days, including times when she has to lock herself in her office and work on budgets or project plans alone, but she also knows it will be important to do what fuels her—working with and helping people—so she can get through those quiet moments in small doses.

Riding into the Sunset…Forever

Now, let's flip the coin.

I met Greg when he was in his early sixties. We did an initial assessment and were digging into the work we planned to do together. We talked about his introversion and I mentioned how it likely helped him to be really successful in this technical field over the years.

That's when Greg started crying. Not just tears in his eyes but sobbing. He was miserable. For decades he fought the "need" to be alone. He enrolled in classes, hired a coach, and finally resorted to finding a doctor who would prescribe anxiety medication. I asked him to back up and start from the beginning.

He slumped over and wrung his hands as he explained that while in high school and college, he really enjoyed the technical and strategy classes. This was back in the day when students were expected to work alone, and he did very well. However, he had to live with five other guys to afford the apartment near the campus. He then looked up and said, "I'll never forget graduating from college, getting on my motorcycle, looking at the moon, and saying to myself, *I never have to talk to anyone again.*"

But reality hit and he had to get a job, and most jobs involve working with other people (again, before "working from home" was a thing). Greg was and is a technical genius, and senior leaders quickly noticed his work. They invited him to present a new idea to investors, and it was quickly approved. Everyone who saw his work was in awe of his abilities, especially at such a young age. Soon after, they said, "We need to promote this guy so he can teach and lead others to be as good and smart as him."

It wasn't long before he was incredibly uncomfortable in this new role. Instead of approaching his supervisor and discussing his level of discomfort with the new position, he enrolled in classes, hired a coach, and started self-medicating. One beer after work became six. As his depression about his new role deepened, six beers at night became a twelve-pack. He then found a doctor and, well, you know the rest of the story.

The promotion to a new position with management responsibilities and his unhappiness about it triggered in Greg the long-held feeling that "something is wrong with me," which was reinforced by his boss, his employees, his wife (the first, second, and third wife). As an introvert who drew his energy from working alone on very technical projects, Greg had been told repeatedly he needed to be more sociable and caring about people. It wasn't that Greg didn't care about his colleagues. He did! But his energy was depleted when he was forced to supervise and interact with them more than the time spent on very specific technical projects.

Greg, like Janet, plowed through. He knew he had a good gig as the CEO of a firm. People and investors were counting on him, and he did his very best to get up and at it every day. The solution for Greg was actually quite simple. He needed validation that his introversion was a gift and allowed him to add tremendous value to the firm. It didn't excuse him from spending time with people, but he could be more purposeful in when and how often he interacted with people. He also learned to count on and trust others to manage some of the members of the team while he focused on the technology and strategy for the future.

I recently heard Greg's company was bought out and he is finally living his dream of riding his motorcycle up and down the coast. After 40+ years of feeling like a square peg in a round hole, Greg is finally living his dream.

The Changing Value of Introversion-Extroversion in U.S. History

We live in a world where the loudest voice wins. Those who speak well get the most attention. Ideas are no longer just based on merit, but how they are packaged and presented. We can point to a very specific time in our history when this shift happened.

Introversion was overwhelmingly prized when our nation was largely an agricultural producing economy with small family farms and very scant industry. Think about it: if you are running a farm with your family, the name of the game is hard, mostly solitary work with only your family in your day-to-day existence. Therefore, introversion was a prized asset. If you were an extrovert who was required to work with very few people, it could have been an excruciating existence. And you probably weren't a very happy farmhand.

Even during the Industrial Revolution, managers were not required or expected to talk to or inspire their employees. It was about getting the work done. Punch the clock in, do the work, punch the clock out. Don't talk, just work.

So, what changed? Marketing and employment competition changed the game.

In the early to mid-1900s, companies switched from promoting a product based on value and practicality (the analytical part of the brain), to marketing products based on an emotional perspective. With more industry, more ways to communicate, more ways to visit different communities and stores, now the average consumer had more choice. The "wow" factor became important. Soap wasn't just about getting clean, it was about making you smell and feel so much better. And with the right soap (or clothes, or hair product, or...) you could get the girl, get the job, and live a lavish life. It was more likely the extroverted sales person/company that sold more products than the introverted sales person/company that simply promoted a product based on data and research.

Transition that theory to the world of employment. With all these people now looking and smelling better, and more people moving from the country to the city and competing for jobs, there was an expectation that people had to look the part. And those who could "sell" themselves typically landed the better role. And those who achieved the more desired positions through their verbal skills were also better positioned to climb the ladder of promotions, leaving many of the people who focused solely on their ability to do the work behind.

Many of the introverted professionals I work with are up for a more considerable challenge than those who are naturally extroverted. Society's expectation is that those in professional positions, and especially those in leadership roles, must be outgoing, able to sell and schmooze customers and investors easily and eagerly.

But not all professionals fit that mold. Some draw their energy instead from more quiet tasks like research and strategic planning. The key is to help coach introverted professionals to understand what fuels them and how to make sure they have enough fuel during each day, while also balancing the more extroverted tasks that remain on their plates.

It's also critically important we look underneath the exterior of someone who looks, dresses, and talks the part, to ensure there is substance underneath.

The sweet spot for everyone on a team is when each person understands their own refueling needs, and those of their team members. When this happens, there's greater understanding and acceptance when someone needs to talk through a problem while another needs time alone in their office to resolve an issue.

Managing What Fuels You

The change to open floor plans and collaborative teamwork is typically an extrovert's dream and an introvert's nightmare. And, because extroverts typically have the loudest voice, this seating structure now permeates almost every industry and office setting. Unfortunately, statistics show introverts who are thrown into these environments have lower productivity. They are exhausted by the constant interruptions.

As a society, we shame the child who wants to sit alone and read a book, or the kid who wants to play video games, or the employee who would much rather stay home than go to the company picnic and participate in forced teambuilding activities. I facilitated a workshop for an optometrist practice and started the session by asking people to answer this question. "How many of you:

A) Were so excited to be here it didn't matter what was presented, you just looked forward to a day of getting to know people in other locations?;

B) Looked at the agenda and looked forward to the topics that were interesting to you?;

C) Dreaded this day from the moment it showed up on your calendar. In fact, it took every ounce of energy to get up, get ready, and show up today?"

When I read the final option, a young optometrist who had been looking at his phone from the minute he sat down jerked his head up so fast I thought it would fly off his shoulders! He discreetly held up his hand, though not high enough to draw attention to himself from anyone behind him. His eyes said it all: "Finally, someone understands me."

The A group, being the vocal people that they are, quickly started commenting that everyone should be excited about today. After all, it's all about teambuilding and getting to know each other. So, I turned the tables a bit and asked them how they feel when they must stare at their computer...all day. Loud groans filled the room.

But this is exactly how the introverts felt about being at the session that day. I asked that everyone please give them some grace when they go off into a corner to check their email or have a meaningful 1:1 conversation with someone. They need a *Refuel Break* to recharge their batteries to come back to the full group.

A *Refuel Break* is a time when you are self-aware and purposeful in how to refuel, not by lashing out at others, but by taking time to do what gives you energy. For many people, that can be done by taking a walk, phoning a friend, or checking their smartphone.

Susan Cain, author of *Quiet; The Power of Introverts in a World that Can't Stop Talking*, recommends people create "Free Trait Agreements," which are agreements with yourself or with others to proactively manage your energy and your introvert/extrovert time. If you're an introvert, this Free Trait Agreement might be with your boss or spouse, that you will attend one social event a week or one a month. Or, if you're an extrovert, your agreement might be with yourself that on days when you must work alone, you will always schedule at least one client meeting or a lunch date.

As with every trait, the bottom line is to understand yourself so you can find your Job Joy. It is critical to understand, accept, and celebrate the value of the person who is the opposite of you on this scale and not shame them into something they are not. Take a few minutes to review and complete the Introversion/Extroversion chart to determine where you fall on this spectrum.

What would make you snap? (Circle all that apply to you)	
• Working in an open environment with constant interruptions. • Explaining a concept to someone who hasn't done their research, read the policy or instructions, or didn't take notes the first time you told them.	• Working on your computer, with no human interaction, all day. • Being forced to learn a new process or technology by reading a 200-page manual.
What is your preference? (Circle all that apply to you)	
• Working alone to solve a problem. • Having a small group of close friends/colleagues. • Making decisions based on facts and research. • Working in a controlled, quiet environment.	• Working with a team to solve a problem. • Having the opportunity to meet new people. • Making decisions based on how it will impact people. • Working in an environment where people are encouraged to talk/collaborate.
If you circled more on this side, you're likely more Introverted	If you circled more on this side, you're likely more Extroverted
Consider Roles	
• That allow you to focus on your work without a lot of interruptions. • With enough like-minded people who appreciate the value of data/research and welcome deep, meaningful conversations. • If in a sales role, the sale should be based on the buyer appreciating the technical aspect of the product, not as much about the social interaction.	• That allow you to work and collaborate with others. • Where you can do work or make decisions that impact people • In which people are encouraged to meet and work face to face and there are times when you can socialize. • If in a sales role, the sale should be based on the relationship, not just the technical aspect or lowest cost.

Ways to stretch yourself	
• When required to be in a social setting, start with the outside perimeter of the room and focus on one or two people with whom you can have a meaningful conversation. • Have one or two go-to questions in mind if someone strikes up a conversation in a large setting. There are numerous books that can help you be prepared. • Be self-aware of when you need a Refuel Break—don't wait until you're on your last nerve and about to unleash on someone.	• If you need to work alone on a project, break it into manageable chunks with human interaction in between. Keep in mind, social media is not human interaction—you need real human interaction, not screen time! • Seek out someone who is standing alone at an event, and instead of dragging them to a bigger group, strike up a meaningful conversation and LISTEN to what they are saying, not just waiting for a break so you can speak next. • Be self-aware of when you need a Refuel Break—don't wait until you can't get off the couch!

Chapter 8

HOW YOU REACT TO SITUATIONS

We all know who to go to when we need someone to fix our problems. And we know those friends who we engage when we need someone who will listen and be empathetic.

Which are you?

If you don't immediately know which group you fall into, ask yourself this question: What is your reaction when the unforeseen happens?

- ° Is your first reaction to fix the problem? Or...
- ° Is your first reaction one of sympathy?

These two opposites are defined as logic versus sensitivity. Regardless of which "side" is your default, most move to the other side after a period of time; for some people the time is short, for others it takes longer. The person who starts with logic will eventually have an emotional reaction. Conversely, the individual who is more sensitive needs time to work through the emotion before applying logic in a situation.

These two extremes played out right in front of my eyes in the spring of 2008. We had just survived a terribly cold winter with record snowfall, followed quickly with a very rainy spring, both in our area and to the north. We were warned of the potential of flooding, and with a city built along a river, this wasn't unusual. We had survived floods in the past, so we all knew the drill…until it rained seven inches in 24 hours! Then all hell and the dams broke loose.

When our city's river first started rising we invited our friends, who lived and owned a business quite a distance from the river, to stay with us until the madness dissipated. We went to the local bar and had pizza and a few drinks, talking with friends and neighbors about the weather and how we would all pitch in to help those who lived close to the river. However, within an hour or two, the noisy bar grew eerily quiet as we all watched in horror as dams and levees broke and the water quickly turned streets into raging rivers.

We got into our cars and drove home in silence.

That's when the "what is your reaction when the unforeseen happens" played out. My husband responds to situations with 100% logic. He is the go-to guy when you need a situation fixed immediately. While he cares tremendously about people, he doesn't get emotional. That night, as we started to realize the impact of the flood, he got out his notepad and pen and started making a list of things to buy at the local hardware store: bleach, scrub brushes, buckets, Lysol, lumber, sheet rock—the list went on and on. Our friends who feared they lost their home and business to the raging waters were still trying to wrap their brains around the situation.

The next day we dodged the National Guard and snuck through backyards and alleys to get to our friends' home to retrieve any possessions we could before the house caved in or the roads were permanently closed. We cleaned out the refrigerator and freezer, grabbed clothes, toiletries, and important insurance and personal documents. All the while, our friends alternated between trying to salvage everything and wanting to run and hide.

While it was important to have people who were taking control to save as many lives and as much property as possible, my daughter, who had worked with people after Hurricane Katrina, knew that it was equally important to exercise great empathy. She excelled at sitting and being with the people who were experiencing trauma, to meet them where they are and listen, and to not pass judgment or start telling them all the things they "should" be doing.

This monumental flood impacted 18,000 residents, including our friends and 42 employees in the business where I worked. Watching the situation unfold at home gave me valuable insight that we needed both the logical and sensitive leaders to help our employees navigate through this horrific disaster.

We assembled a team of "ambassadors," employees who would partner 1:1 with their colleagues who were hardest hit by the flood, to act as their counselor and coach and to find resources when they were needed. Others were organizing teams to raise money and put together "Home Kits" that included all the items needed in a new home, when that time came for our 42 employees. Still other employees volunteered at the animal shelter to help pets that had been unfortunately stranded or needed a temporary home. When the unforeseen happened, people did what they were best at doing to help those in need.

If they would just...

The "if they would just..." phrase is usually followed by a statement that resembles "...be more like me." The person who says, "if they would just be more sensitive" is usually a more sensitive and empathetic person. And the one you often hear emphatically stating, "if they would just be more logical and less sensitive" is likely the person who approached a situation with logic and can seem detached emotionally.

The logic-empathy trait is often misunderstood. People on either side can become extremely frustrated with the other. The logical side views the sensitive group as too emotional, and the sensitive group sees the logical group as too detached. And, through their lens, they both feel they are right. And just as importantly, they are both needed.

We need both logic and sensitivity in every aspect of life and business. Consider how we parent and teach our children, our marketing and sales campaigns, and creating technology and apps. If we were to approach any of these things purely from a logic and detached standpoint, we'd treat kids like soldiers and have marketing, sales, and technology tools that might work efficiently, but won't win the heart and souls of consumers.

Conversely, if we only approached situations with sympathy and empathy, we'd often miss the logical steps to resolve a problem or work through a process.

In the past, heralded business leaders were those who made decisions only based on logic, never emotion. I have worked with leaders who were all logic, as well as a couple who made every decision based on emotion. The extremes no longer work in today's society, and some would argue they didn't work well in the past! The sweet spot is when the leader possesses high self-awareness to understand when a situation calls for logic and when it calls for being sensitive to listen to and understand the emotional needs of others. This is often seen as high emotional intelligence, and it is proven to be one of the key indicators of leadership effectiveness.

There are two short YouTube videos that hit to the nail on the head, pun intended, when it comes to understanding this topic. I encourage you to view them in the following order:

- "It's Not About the Nail" illustrates approaching a situation with logic versus sensitivity/emotion;
- "Brene' Brown on Empathy" does a great job illustrating empathy, especially for those logical people who may view empathy as sympathy or pity.

A few years ago, I worked with the CEO of a nonprofit. She was promoted through the ranks very quickly due to her strong business sense. After working with her team, we both realized just how vastly different she is from the rest of her team. Her first reaction to almost every situation is with logic and a business strategy. Not surprisingly for a social service organization, everyone else—and I mean EVERYONE else—on her team reacts first with sensitivity and emotion. Having this awareness was critical in building a stronger team. She knew she needed to rely on them for sensitive issues and how to present projects and programs to meet the needs of the employees and clients. They knew she was someone they could go to if they needed to step back and take a more logical approach to a situation.

Think of it this way:

- The more logical person shows empathy by helping people fix their issue.
- The more sensitive person shows empathy in the more traditional meaning of the word by their capacity to sit and listen.

One final coaching tip for those who are more logical than sensitive: When someone is in crisis, the very first reaction shouldn't be to try and fix it or get people to see the bright side. Case in point, when my father passed away, a well friend, whose father deserted her family at a young age, said to me, "That's too bad your father died, but at least you had a good father." While I understood that she was trying to "silver line" the situation, I was not comforted by this. Sadly, this wasn't an isolated incident. A few years later when my mother passed away after a very long illness, many well-intentioned friends and colleagues said to me, "I'm sorry your mother died, but at least she's no longer in pain." A true statement that I possibly said a time or two about my mother. However, it's not a statement that should be made to someone who lost someone close. An empathetic statement never includes "but at least." When in doubt on what to say to someone who is suffering, acknowledge their pain and just be with that person.

On a lighter note, a final tip on how to tell a logical person from a sensitive one. When someone tells a funny joke, the sensitive person freely laughs out loud. While the logical person will often respond with, "that's hilarious" and freely laughs on the inside.

There's a time for logic and a time for sensitivity. The key, as is true with every personality trait, is to understand your natural way and to know when to stretch and/or call on others who are stronger in that trait, when needed. Check out the chart below to evaluate your place on the logic–empathy spectrum.

What would make you snap? (Circle all that apply to you)	
• Listening to people's problems without the ability to take action to fix it. • Interacting with a preponderance of people/clients who have emotional reactions to situations. • Requiring that you share your emotions with the expectation a good leader/professional should occasionally cry.	• Working closely with someone who feels emotions do not belong in the workplace. • Making all decisions based purely on logic that seem impersonal. • Requiring you never show your emotion.
What is your preference? (Circle all that apply to you)	
• Being in a business role, where confidence and logic are rewarded.	• Appreciation for spontaneity, laughter, and making it safe to show sadness.
If you circled more on this side, you're likely more Logical/Detached	If you circled more on this side, you're likely more Sensitive/Intuitive
Consider Roles	
• Where confidence and logic are the bases for decisions. • Where emotions are detrimental to a positive outcome.	• That require high empathy/sympathy, such as jobs with children, those with mental or physical disabilities. • Marketing or service roles that require you understand the emotional need of the client.
Ways to stretch yourself	
• Recognizing when someone is in distress, take the time to listen and just "be" with the person. Restrain from wanting to "fix" the situation.	• In situations where emotional reactions may make the situation worse, practice taking three deep breaths. • When someone has been stuck in a situation for too long, learn when to ask questions that can help him or her to move forward.

Chapter 9

ARE YOU THE TORTOISE OR THE HARE?

Now let's talk about your relationship with time. And by this, I don't mean whether you're constantly running ten minutes behind or are always five minutes early. These days, none of us seem to have enough time in the day. Twenty-four hours isn't always enough for us to accomplish our personal and professional to-do lists.

But that's not what I mean when I say "time."

Instead, I define "time" as the way and manner in which you process information, your work, and the world around you. While it's scientifically proven no brain can multitask, some people can switch gears so wickedly fast it appears that they can. Conversely, some prefer to focus on one task or project at a time until it is completed, or at a logical stopping point.

A perfect example of the latter is Zach, a phenomenal computer programmer. He had been known and respected within his company for his knowledge as well as sticking with a project until it was finished. He loved to conduct research to understand the whole issue, map out a plan for how to move forward, and then immerse himself into making it happen. He was so calm and patient. Nothing got Zach off-track.

In fact, he was so good, he got—yep, you guessed it—promoted to a supervisor position. As a supervisor of a small team he still had a handful of projects, but more than half of his day was spent bouncing from meeting to meeting, with little time in between. He was expected to return emails within two hours and juggle not only his projects, but also the entire team's projects. Zach went from being a patient programmer who worked flawlessly on long-term projects to feeling overwhelmed and a failure for not being able to juggle multiple priorities. Some co-workers decided "he has no sense of urgency" and others called him slow.

Once you understand the two extremes, you will see someone like Zach as "methodical." In order to be successful and his best, Zach needs to understand the context of a situation, not just the headline or the punch line. He needs to understand what happened up to this point so he can determine the process to get to the end goal. Zach is not a "shoot from the hip" kind of guy, and when answering a question he'll provide you with the information that led up to this point. And if you think there's no need for these types of people in our world, what kind of surgeon would you want to perform an eight-hour highly intricate surgery? Would you prefer the surgeon who gets bored easily, or the one who loves to immerse herself into her "project" until it is done perfectly to the end? Conversely, a busy emergency room would benefit by having a doctor that revels in moving quickly from one patient to the next, making equally fast, sound decisions.

As we discussed in the chapter about creativity, there is a push in this world for everyone to be "outside the box thinkers." Similarly, in today's society there's an assumption we should all operate at 100 mph.

Given the break-neck speed of life, the general societal belief is that we should all be able to focus on multiple computer screens, respond to emails and text messages within thirty seconds, and juggle twenty balls in the air at a time.

Is this realistic? For some, yes. These high sense of urgency people thrive in this environment! Some may even refer to them as adrenaline junkies; they are go, go, goers. They are at their best when their plate is full and they have a lot of irons in the fire. They get bored easily if they must spend too much time on one thing for too long.

But not everyone is an adrenaline junkie who thrives in a fast-paced environment! Some people must immerse themselves in whatever they are doing until they either finish it or hit a logical stopping point. When they are interrupted it takes effort to unwind from what they are doing, wind into the next thing, then unwind, and rewind back to the original thing.

Darla left her job at a fast-paced for-profit organization to take a job with a governmental agency. One of Darla's amazing strengths is her ability to handle thirteen different cases at one time—while putting out seven unrelated fires. She can jump from one case to the next to the next, all without batting an eye. She was spectacular at managing caseloads and administering benefits. When she chose to leave her place of employment, I was shocked. But she said she wanted a change of scenery and felt her talents would be well utilized at a governmental agency. She was bringing considerable years' worth of experience to a smaller team.

Darla and I connected for lunch a few months after she started at the agency. I could tell something was off. She had gained some weight and the fire in her eyes had been extinguished. We made small talk for a while and she said her new job was "fine" when I asked about it.

But then it was like a pressure valve finally released and she said the red tape within the agency was killing her. She was still working at her rapid-fire pace, but it wasn't well received in the new environment. The supervisors in the departments downstream didn't appreciate being inundated with the cases she was quickly pushing through, and they felt she didn't provide enough context for them to take the proper next step. Essentially, her sense of urgency and quick pace was not welcome in an agency that was accustomed to working much more methodically.

Congratulations to Darla for recognizing so quickly what was happening in her new job. Thankfully, Darla's former employer wanted her back and she returned with a new appreciation for the green grass on her original side of the fence.

It is easy to become frustrated with someone who has a different natural pace than you. The key is in understanding that some people may have a super high sense of urgency while others have a natural methodical pace. And telling someone they must "slow down" or "speed up" is rarely a successful long-term solution.

My husband, Dan, and I are a textbook case of two individuals who have a different natural pace. I'm thankful that we are cognizant of these differences, which allow us to navigate everyday conversations as well as difficult decisions.

At night Dan can surf the web, watch a TV show, switch to answering a quick text, listen in to the conversation behind him, and then fire off a question to me.

While no one has accused me of being overly patient, relative to my husband there's quite a delta in our styles. As I sit on the sofa, immersed in a project and his question comes flying my direction, I hold up a finger and say, "Hold that thought, let me finish this and I'll come back to you." Once I have reached a good stopping point, I pause and give him my full attention. Usually by this point he has moved on or answered the question himself.

Dan and I are both self-employed. He is a realtor and he is happiest when he has numerous clients in all stages of the sales and buying process. On the other hand, I thrive best when I have a handful of clients with whom I work on long-term projects. There's a definite need for both personality types in the world. In today's real estate market, if a realtor isn't responding quickly the client may lose out on the house of their dreams. In my world of consulting on "people issues," there is rarely a quick fix.

Most of us have heard Aesop's Fable of the Tortoise and the Hare. It has always been one of my favorites, long before I started paying attention to people's pace and sense of urgency. To refresh your memory, the speedy hare arrogantly ridicules the slow but steady tortoise. Annoyed, the tortoise challenges the hare to a race. At the start, the hare jumps out to a commanding lead and begins to do things other than focus on the race (multi-task), while the tortoise stays immersed in his one job of finishing the race.

In the classic fable, the tortoise wins. However, we see repeatedly in today's world there isn't just one animal that always wins the race. Today there is a race and a place for hares and tortoises! There's a need for methodical people who will think through and stick with long-term projects. We also need people who can make quick decisions and operate in a high sense of urgency.

Take a moment to review your Job Joy tool and your relationship with time, keeping in mind we need a world balanced with tortoises and hares!

What would make you snap? (Circle all that apply to you)	
• Being required to work on one project for a long period of time. • Serving in a role where taking your time and patience was required. • Working with no interruptions, for introverts this might be the constant pinging of texts or emails and for extroverts this might be constant people stopping by or asking questions.	• Constant interruptions and no time to finish a project. • A schedule that required you go from one meeting to the next, with no time to immerse yourself in what is important to you. • Someone constantly saying, "Hurry up, you have to move/ switch gears faster".
What is your preference? (Circle all that apply to you)	
• Multiple projects. • Quick wins • Operating .at a high sense of urgency.	• Planning your own schedule and no one interrupting it. • Focusing on your priority until it is finished.
If you circled more on this side, you're likely more Quick Pace/Inpatient	If you circled more on this side, you're likely more Methodical/Patient
Consider Roles	
• Where you can make quick decisions. • Where thinking on your feet is rewarded. • Where you can juggle multiple, quick priorities. • Where many others around you have the same sense of urgency.	• Where patience and methodical work is expected and respected. • Where you are encouraged to stick with a project until it is finished. • Where you can schedule the "just in time" issues that have to be handled, i.e.: emails, questions.

Ways to stretch yourself	
• Make sure a large part of your day is spent at a lightning-fast pace, and schedule short periods of time when you work on your projects that require more attention or working with a colleague that has a more methodical pace. Forcing yourself to stick with it or forcing that person to "hurry up" will have a quick diminishing rate of return. • When you feel anxious that the pace is too slow, remove yourself from the situation. You are likely putting a lot of pressure on yourself and everyone around you. Take a walk, go for a run, knock out some emails—get it out of your system so you can be more patient.	• Make sure a large part of your day is spent working on projects that are important to you and identify logical stopping points—you may not get to the end. • Schedule times to respond to emails, voicemails, and questions. The more you put them off, the more the person on the other end will get frustrated. • Because you tend to ponder a question before answering, make sure you have some "go-to" statements for those who want a quick answer, such as, "To make sure I give you the right answer, I would like to work that through and get back with you tomorrow." This won't work for every situation, but often it can buy you time.

Chapter 10

KEEPING YOUR RUBBER BAND HAPPY

At the beginning of this journey together, you were challenged to reflect on a time when you were at your best and a time you were at your lowest. Before we go any further, now is a great time to look back at that list, as well as the charts you completed after each chapter. Really study it and find the patterns and correlations.

If you're feeling great about your situation, congratulations! This is usually when people are flying so high they don't take time to do an inventory on life. But, that's not you! You read this book and you know how important this work is! In fact, now is the perfect time to deeply assess what is going well. Be as specific as possible, so when, or if, you start to feel "off," you will have this list to reflect on.

If your career is not feeling like a happy rubber band, do any of these resonate with you?

- Are you an extrovert that is living in an introvert role? Or vice versa?

- Are you a more agreeable person in a high-risk role like sales? Or an assertive person that is bored by the predictability of your job?
- Are you feeling anxious because there's pressure to pick up the pace, or conversely in a role that your go-go self is constantly being told to slow down?

If you get a pain in your stomach, head, or heart when you think about work, please don't immediately fire off a resignation notice. Rather, take a step back and identify which specific part is causing you stress and decide if there are adjustments you can make. If you miss this step, you may jump right into another ill-suited role. For instance:

1) If you're an introvert in an extrovert's world, inquire if you can work from a quieter cube where you don't have to listen to all of the chatter. Can you work from home a few days a week? Or, consider talking with your boss or coworker (or spouse) about a Free Trait Agreement (see page 52).

2) Are you an extrovert and work from home, find meaningful reasons to go into the office on a regular basis. If you're a solo entrepreneur, consider renting a coworking space or work a few hours at a coffee shop (just remember to buy a cup of Joe while you're there and not just free-load off the Wi-Fi), where you will likely run into people you know. Schedule lunch dates or meetings and consider joining a club, such as Rotary, Toast Masters, or a nonprofit board—all have the foundation of talking and building relationships. It's a huge bonus if the meetings are in the morning or during the day. If you join a club that meets at night you may be so exhausted from working alone all day you won't be able to get off the couch!

3) Do you NEED to take control but are in a role that doesn't allow for your assertiveness? Consider taking on a volunteer leadership role or ask to lead a special assignment or work group. Just make sure it's meaningful and not a "check the box" type of activity.

4) If you're in a sales role and like to work with people but would rather poke out your eyes than get one more rejection, consider transitioning to a sales support or customer service role. You may lose your commissions, but you may gain your strength and sanity.

5) If you're super creative and in a "stay in the box" role, consider volunteering to review a process that isn't working, either at your office or with a non-profit.

6) Do you feel like you're not good enough because all of these creative, brainstorming crazy people are making you feel like you're stuck? Consider being the note-taker and researching to see if you can find others who have already implemented a proposed new idea so you can learn best practices from them.

7) In a role you hate but it is required to get to the one you want? Hopefully you have a supervisor who understands personality traits and that this role may be difficult for you. But keep in mind, this is your issue, not your supervisor's. You accepted this role, and you have to decide to either make it work or move on. If you elect the former, take the time to understand the requirements, vow to meet those requirements, and be purposeful to engage in refueling activities outside the office that align with your natural traits so you don't lose passion.

8) If you have over-extended yourself trying to be everything to everyone, remember these things about saying "no":

a) You have the right to say no.
b) No one will say no for you.
c) Saying no doesn't equal failure or quitting. It allows you to say yes to the things that fuel you.
d) If you're saying no due to fear, take a few minutes to evaluate the risk. This may be a stretch moment, not a snap moment.

9) Apply the Golden Rule to yourself. Treat yourself the way you want to be treated. Often, we encourage a friend or family member to do what brings them joy, but we don't allow ourselves the same grace. And while we're talking about the Golden Rule, do not apply it to others. We need to treat others the way THEY want to be treated, which is often different than how we want to be treated.

All Done, Right? Nope!

If we stopped with the knowledge and the immediate plan, things would be good...for a while. But just like putting your time and energy into physically being healthy, things can go badly quickly if you don't make a commitment to continuously monitor yourself.

Undoubtedly, there will be events that can get you off-track with your newly minted knowledge and plan. There are roadblocks out there waiting to pop up! I refer to it as "Work-Life Whack-A-Mole." If you're of a certain generation (like me!) who fondly remembers crowded arcades that smelled of burnt popcorn and featured games like Skee Ball and Pop-A-Shot, then you surely recall Whack-A-Mole. It's a silly game where you have a mallet, and every time the annoying mole pops up it's your job to whack him back down into his hole. But he's relentless, and he pops up when you least expect it. Over and over again. To be successful, you must be vigilant and a diligent. You must be prepared that when you feel you are getting off course, you are ready with your figurative mallet.

Every. Single. Time.

Let's talk about some of the real-life "Whack-A-Mole" things that can pull you off-track. Some may be very familiar to you!

Beware of the Outside Voices

There are so many voices out there!

The Over-Positive Voice

The over-positive voice that says: "You're so good at 'x' you should do 'y.'" You may even be telling yourself this!

Before proceeding with this section, please know I am all for positive reinforcement, encouragement, and sometimes giving people that little extra "you can do this" so they will give it a try. We grow the most when we take a chance to see what we are capable of doing (STRETCH). This section is about being purposeful and vigilant.

Before you make the leap into a new role because other outside voices believe you are infallible, it's imperative you have a realistic understanding of your strengths and weaknesses in your particular work role. Yes, it's awesome to stretch! That's when we are at our best—our rubber bands are happy when stretched for a period of time! You must also be honest with yourself about what is working and what is not working in your current role. Are the things that bring you joy and energy also found in this new role? Will there at least be enough

"Refuel Breaks" (see page 52) or someone who is open to your "Free Trait Agreement"? (see page 52)

Back in the day when someone was promoted beyond his or her capability, we called it the Peter Principle. Essentially, you've hit the Peter Principle when you've been promoted so much you are in over your head. The traits, skills, and competencies which made you successful in the past don't translate to the new role. The Peter Principle can happen slowly over several positions, or quickly with one promotion. You can avoid this happening if you think critically about your strengths and weaknesses instead of blindly listening to the outside voices that say, "You could do any job at this company!"

My friend Tom was a technical genius. Because everything he touched on the technical side of our company turned to gold, the entire leadership team wanted to elevate him to a role with more management responsibilities. After months of flattery from everyone in the C-Suite and them saying, "You should take this new role," Tom accepted the position.

The challenge, however, was Tom doesn't draw his energy from people. In his technical role, he was congenial and always engaged because he spent most of his day working primarily alone on his very specific duties. Once he was "promoted," he spent most of his day in meetings and explaining things, sometimes multiple times. Over a few weeks he came in every day and into every meeting with his hoodie pulled over his head, slumped over his phone or computer, avoiding eye contact with anyone. Management noticed and quickly deduced "something must be going on" with Tom in his personal life. No one considered it was the change in work role which altered his behavior so significantly!

After a few months of Tom underperforming, management decided to remove his management responsibilities. Not surprisingly, almost overnight, the old Tom came back. One day I was in the office and he voluntarily stopped by, hood off, said "Hi" and asked if I could stop by when I had a few minutes. The transformation was so quick and dramatic! Everyone else noticed, too, and assumed that Tom was "fixed." So, they did what most management teams would do...they moved Tom back into people management. Unfortunately, but not surprisingly, the same behaviors happened again. Can you hear Tom's rubber band? *SNAP!*

Tom's story is a good reminder that you must be careful when people are "should-ing" on you. When your colleague says, "You should submit that proposal" or "You should apply for that opening," be wary. There is no doubt people intend these statements as compliments, but think hard before making them your own personal road map.

The Over-Negative Voice

While it can be dangerous to believe in your own hype, it can be equally as damaging if you start to believe the negative things people say about you or you continually say about or to yourself.

These are the people who tell you you're not good enough; their "should-ing" has a very negative slant. Phrases such as, "You should be more organized," "You should be more assertive," "You should be more sociable." In their eyes you are never good enough. You start to believe something is wrong with you.

Let me introduce you to Grace. Grace is incredibly bright, talented, and very well respected in her profession. For some reason, Grace's boss went from nominating her for every company award imaginable and being her "best friend" to making her life miserable, talking behind her back, and sabotaging her work relations. Grace was at an all-time low and really frustrated. She and I and another friend were having coffee, and we started talking about the voices in your head that can lift you up or take you down—akin to the angel on one shoulder and the devil on the other. We all agreed you need to know when to knock that devil off your shoulder.

This obviously struck a chord—or a nerve—with Grace and she quickly stood up and said, "You know what? I'm going to flick that bitch!" And with her middle finger and thumb pressed firmly together, she reached up to her shoulder, flicked that imaginary devil off her shoulder, and marched out of that coffee shop with a newfound confidence. Best. Moment. Ever!

Feedback is a gift—one that we should thank upon receipt, examine it closely, and decide if it is helpful and we should keep it, or if it is harmful and we should pitch it. Now, if you have heard this feedback from others, give it extra attention before deciding to pitch it. If the person giving the feedback is someone who has your back and you believe they care about you personally and professionally, you're likely to take that feedback more seriously. But if that feedback becomes the voice in your head that says you're not good enough for anyone or anything, it is time to stand up, flick that bitch and move forward! Do NOT let the negative voice define you!

Your Parents' Voice

If I had written this book thirty years ago, I would not have written a section urging my readers to live their dreams and not the dreams their parents have for them. But this is 2020, not 1990.

A lot has happened in society in those intervening years.

We now have Helicopter Parents who constantly hover, and may, for instance, call their son while at college to ensure he wakes up in time for class. And we have Bulldozer Parents, who make sure all obstacles are removed so their child has an easy path and who may, for instance, take over their daughter's third grade science projects, or years down the road pay to have their daughter's ACT scores changed to get them into a more prestigious school. Or the aggressive parent on the soccer field or in the bleachers yelling at the referees, coaches, and other players on their child's behalf.

I'm not a social scientist, but there are obvious factors creating these new parental archetypes:

- Parent(s) are having fewer children later in life, so the few they have get more attention than their prior generations of more kids/family;
- Apps allow us to track every move our child makes;
- Social media and the media in general are putting a big spotlight on those who have high academic and athletic achievements, thus ratcheting up the pressure on everyone;
- Our children learn and practice active shooter drills, which makes parents even more protective;
- Every parent from every generation wants to make their child's life better and easier than their own.

I want to first add, thank goodness, the first few points did not apply to my generation. We were allowed to run, play, get in trouble, make mistakes, and push the line—quite often over the edge.

However, we are where we are, and as a result, many parents are overly protective and more involved than ever in their kids' lives.

As you progress in the work environment—whether you were raised by a Helicopter Parent, a Bulldozer Parent, or just a parent who was trying to provide good advice, or none of the above—remember you exist to fulfill your dreams, not anyone else's. This is your life, and as long as it is not illegal, immoral, or unethical, please stay true to who you are and your dreams. And as a side note, the longer you live in your parents' home, ask/accept money from them, and/or stay on their insurance, the more they will feel they have the right to tell you what to do!

And, if you have kids (and believe me, there's a little self-talk in here as well), let your kids be kids. Let them play and dream. Let them make mistakes without encasing them in bubble wrap. When they get older they will likely not land the perfect job in high school or right after college. They need some crappy jobs to appreciate the good ones. We all know the most beautiful roses grow with a healthy dose of fertilizer (aka manure/crap). While guidance is good, pressure and "should-ing" on them can quickly make them second-guess themselves and make career decisions that are ill-suited

Keep Your Finances in Check

Another thing that can knock you off track is getting caught up in the lure of money or getting into serious debt. The height of my career was in the dot-com era, and I worked for a dot-com-type company. Many believed everything we touched turned to gold and the promotions and bonuses were deserved and would last forever. Until they didn't. We were hit hard, but others were hit harder. People overextended themselves. They took on big mortgages, second homes, and fancy cars because surely the money would always be there. Until it wasn't.

There is serious danger in getting into a spot where you can't leave your job because you have a lifestyle you need to maintain. It is at this point you are most susceptible to make bad decisions about your career. If a promotion is dangled in front of you and you feel like you absolutely MUST take it in order to support your lifestyle, even if the position is a bad fit, then you're chasing the money and there's a good chance that race will end badly.

Conversely, I understand sometimes you must take the job that pays more because you are living paycheck to paycheck. There was a time early in my career when, as a single mom on a modest income, I would sit down and decide which bill didn't get paid that month. I vividly remember the day we didn't qualify for free and reduced lunches (though I was too damn proud to ever enroll). I often took a new job because it paid 10% more—that was at least two to three years of average merit increases. Money is a motivator when you are trying to meet your basic needs, and sometimes you must decide, "Will I take a job that pays more even if the other brings me greater Job Joy?" Your or your kids' growling stomach will quite often win that battle. I pray both Job Joy and finances can align sooner rather than later. I also pray when you're in a more comfortable financial decision you always choose the path that brings you greater Job Joy.

Think back to earlier in the book when I asked you to define when you had the greatest Job Joy. Was it based solely on money? Were the times when you were at your best the day you got a big commission check or bonus? And if it was, was it the check itself, or do you more fondly remember the work it took to earn it? Some of the happiest people in the world live the most austere lifestyles. And some of the unhappiest people live lavish lifestyles. While money does provide the basics and allows you flexibility and stability, the adage "money doesn't buy happiness" has lived on for so many generations for a reason. And, trust me, the older you get the better you'll understand this.

Keep Your Ego in Check

Jim, my boss for nearly twenty years, used to say, "Don't read your own press clippings." This was back in the day when we got our news on paper newspapers and a lot of the press was about incredible achievements. "Press clippings" highlight what you achieved in the past, and it's gratifying to relish in the moment and celebrate. The key is "for a moment." Most people start to lose their competitive edge when they only read and believe the good stuff and miss the warning signs that your amazingness is slipping. These signs usually start small and are overlooked or brushed off until they are big and someone is now making the headline and getting all the press.

Your ego makes you believe you can do anything.

Your ego talks you into believing only you deserve the next promotion. The next big sale. The next whatever.

Your ego says you are better than anyone else.

Your ego convinces you that you don't have to work as hard because "you got this."

Your ego will make you believe you deserve all the glory and can do it alone.

And this, my friends, is when someone or something will knock you off your egotistical pedestal. And the people you have cast aside because they didn't subscribe to your greatness or because you thought you could do it alone may not be rushing in to help you.

Listen to the Tim McGraw's song "Always Stay Humble and Kind" and let someone else read your press clippings. You have more hard work to do.

Choose Your Boss Wisely

You may have just said to yourself, "But I don't get to choose my boss."

Au, contraire! We do, ultimately, get to decide whom we work for. Showing up for work every day is a choice. Working for the company you work for is a choice. If you are working for someone who doesn't care about you or views employees as commodities, then you have a choice: continue in an untenable situation or find another job.

I have been blessed to have worked for some of the absolute best (thank you, Art, Jim, Joe, and Linda) and some of the absolute worst. Contrary to what Instagram wants us all to believe, no relationship is perfect and all take some work. If you are struggling with your boss, try to understand his or her authentic traits and identify strategies to improve your communication and working relationship. Some managers are open to feedback, and it's always best to try to work things out before moving on. Just remember, the only person you can change is yourself, and you have to understand by looking at your boss' patterns of behavior to assess if it's worth sticking around.

By the end of your career, you will likely have amassed the good and the bad bosses. Hopefully more of the former than the latter. I have worked for a paranoid leadership team that one day conducted an espionage sweep—that certainly did not win the hearts and souls of anyone in the organization. There was also the boss who I walked up to in the hallway to ask a question who didn't even acknowledge my existence, but instead tapped harder on her iPad before briskly walking into her office and slamming the door shut. I wondered for a moment if I was completely invisible. It took a long time for me to realize her behaviors were a reflection on her, not me. She was an introvert, and anyone interrupting her thought process was too much to handle. She had to go to her office to refuel. Yet, as a new employee, that was not helpful.

At some point in your life, I hope you experience working with a great boss (and that you are a great manager yourself) who takes the time to understand your personality and strengths, who encourages and respects you, and challenges you. A boss who listens, takes the time to get to know you and your family (without wanting to be besties), and gives you meaningful feedback. The great boss isn't perfect, and you definitely won't think exactly alike. In fact, you will likely have disagreements and professional debates and conversations. I was at my best when I worked for someone who was quite different than me, yet there was a mutual respect: me for his conservative, introverted ways, and he for my extroverted, not always the best organized, risk-taking self. We balanced each other incredibly well, and while I pushed us to take more risks, he reined me in when I was getting too close to the edge. Irritated the hell out of me at times, but overall it worked great.

No one achieves great success alone. It takes a village, and I am eternally grateful to the great bosses, mentors, and the amazing, caring people who I worked with over the years! Heck, even the turds will teach you a fair amount on how NOT to treat people.

The headline is this: The person you work for will play a significant role to make or break your future. If you work for someone who doesn't care, who doesn't get it, or who doesn't have your back and support you, it will be that much harder to grow and find Job Joy.

Put on Your Oxygen Mask First

The safety reminder on airplanes should be universal. Be kind to yourself. How you feel matters. If something is off, take the time to figure it out, because it impacts every part of and every person in your life. If you hear yourself saying or thinking one of these comments, it should be a red flag you need to check your rubber band:

- "It's called 'work' for a reason."
- "Suck it up, buttercup."
- "That Job Joy stuff is just for hippies/millennials/people who don't work."
- "I heard Essential Oils can lift me out of this funk." (I have a cabinet full of EOs from my transition years if you'd like to stop by!)
- "I have pain in my head/neck/back/heart/stomach that no one can explain."

And PS: If you're talking with friends or colleagues and someone says any of the above phrases, this could be code for "I'm miserable, this is my mantra, so everyone else should subscribe to it as well." When we are in a bad spot our defense mechanism is to become more hardened toward ourselves and others, and we often exhibit an undertone of anger you wouldn't normally associate with that person.

As I mentioned earlier, approach managing your career as a lifestyle, not a fad or a "diet." Just like a diet, with focus and hard work we can achieve a role that fits you just right. But if you manage your career like a "diet" and not a lifestyle change, you'll fall off the wagon and wake up one day wondering what happened.

To maintain Job Joy, reassess where you are at specific times:

- **At a designated time each year.** This might be on New Year's, your birthday, an annual vacation when you have some quiet time, or when you change the clock and "spring forward." Pick a time each year and commit to yourself that you're going to revisit or redo your Job Joy worksheet.

- **When considering a job change.** Our ego can expand very quickly when we hear, "Hey, you should apply for this job, you'd be great at it and it pays more, has a better title, more prestige, bigger office…" Do your homework! Does this new role build on your traits? Are you more attracted to the money than the work? Who will be your boss and how much do you know about them?

- **When you hear yourself saying, "It's called work for a reason," "Suck it up, buttercup," "Is there an Essential Oil for this?" or "What is this ache that no one can explain?"** These are all warning signs you need to reassess some part of your life!

The key is to be vigilant and diligent in sticking to your plan.

Conclusion

Fifteen years after that third-grade assignment, I found myself at a grown-up desk at a family department store. Over the prior four years, I held jobs as a bank teller and receptionist and was now a secretary for a human resources department. My hairstyle matured from pigtails to a more professional bob, and my desk was now an adult size metal desk with drawers on each side to hold everything a twenty-something needed to be successful. I still had three recesses a day, now called breaks and a lunch hour, and I really liked my coworkers.

After a few weeks in the job, my supervisor invited me into her office to congratulate me on my promotion, for which I had not applied. She had terminated the payroll and benefits coordinator, and because I sat in the area (and learned through osmosis?) and because she felt I had potential, she offered me this position. Did I mention I knew nothing about payroll or benefits and had only taken an accounting course at a community college? Over the weekend, I turned over every drawer in that metal desk for some insight on how to ensure 500 people got paid the following week. It was tough, and there were a few manual checks that had to be issued, but everyone got paid and each week got easier and easier!

That is how I "fell" into HR. Over the next 25 years I held every position in this profession, with more success in roles that required critical thinking and strategy than as a payroll and benefits administrator. But through perseverance, driven by a need to pay the mortgage and feed my kids, I was able to "suck it up" to a level of competence. And when money wasn't as great of a motivator, I gave more consideration to jobs and assignments that brought me joy, not just a bigger paycheck. Of course, there was that one time I took a different HR job that ended quite miserably. However, I learned from it. In fact, it made me even more passionate about what I do, and I moved on to greater things.

For me, the "what I want to be" was fairly easy: human resources. It was only when I combined this with the "how I have to be" — creatively guiding people to find their Job Joy—that I discovered Job Joy!

Now, go back and grab that rubber band and really assess where you currently are with your career. Are you happy and fulfilled or do you know there is something better out there for you?

If you're currently not stretched at all, commit you're going to get up and push yourself. No one has ever described their greatest joy as when they went to work late, left early, and had zero challenges in between. Yet, isn't it funny that many of us often wish for the "easy" button? It's a trap, don't fall in. We all need purpose. We need a reason to get up and make a difference. Complacency is the devil's playground.

If you're currently stretched and feel like you're going to snap any moment… First of all, congratulations for taking time to hit the pause button! You obviously know if you stay in this spot you are going to snap, and you and others around you will feel the pain. Maybe your friends or family are asking if you're okay. Or maybe they have asked for so long they have stopped. Often the people who know us and love us can easily see we're in a bad spot long before we can see or feel it ourselves. This is especially true with the "I'll-just-find-a-logical-way-to-work-through-this" person. It's time to set your logic and ego aside and listen to your friends, family, body, and inner voice.

And if you are blessed and your career is that happy little rubber band, alternating between being stretched, getting rest, and spending a whole lot of time in your happy zone—congratulations! There is likely a glow and peace about you others can see and feel. You have probably also discovered the more you stretch and snap back, the <u>farther</u> you can stretch and snap back, just like a real rubber band. And remember, this is the perfect time to take inventory on what is happening at this moment to make you feel this way. Get as specific as possible: which task, project, and interaction (or lack thereof) makes you the most joyful?

Regardless of where you are, know *Discovering Job Joy* is a journey, not a destination. The goal is to be mindful and purposeful in moving forward, which may occasionally require you take a step back. Just don't stay back there for too long!

Like any journey, *Discovering Job Joy* starts with the first step: "What do you want to be?" The second step is discovering, "How do you have to be?" Dig deep and answer this yourself. What makes you happy? When are you at your best? What are you drawn to so strong that you can't stop yourself from doing it? What do you find so easy you just assume it's not that special, or believe that others don't see value in it? This is about getting to the core of who you are, what makes you feel fulfilled, and what brings you joy!

Life is too short. Relationships are too precious. You are too important to put Job Joy off one more day!

You deserve Job Joy!

About the Author

Before starting her own consulting business, Patti Seda worked in a variety of industries, including advertising and marketing, insurance and banking. Starting as a payroll and benefits coordinator, Patti worked her way up to the executive team level in organizations that experienced high growth, as well as business and cultural change. Patti is an accomplished business leader who understands the challenges and opportunities of talent and how it impacts the bottom line. Patti is married, the mother of two school administrators and an entrepreneur, and grandmother to three little girls, all who continuously push and challenge her way of thinking. In 2008, she started a summer youth camp to inspire middle school students to be community leaders. While she established a work ethic growing up on a farm in rural Iowa, her adult life has been involved in business and coaching people and teams to be their best and successful beyond what they believe is possible.